MW01028352

NOTES

including
- *Life and Background*
- *Structure and Narrative Technique*
- *List of Narrator-Characters*
- *Analysis and Commentary*
- *Critical Notes*
- *Notes on Main Characters*
- *Review Questions and Theme Topics*
- *Selected Bibliography*

by
James L. Roberts, Ph.D.
Department of English
University of Nebraska

THIRD EDITION

INCORPORATED

LINCOLN, NEBRASKA   68501

Editor

Gary Carey, M.A.
University of Colorado

Consulting Editor

James L. Roberts, Ph.D.
Department of English
University of Nebraska

ISBN 0-8220-0210-8
© Copyright 1967, 1969
by
C. K. Hillegass
All Rights Reserved
Printed in U.S.A.

1992 Printing

Cliffs Notes, Inc.   Lincoln, Nebraska

CONTENTS

Life and Background 5

Structure and Narrative Technique 7

List of Narrator-Characters 9

Analysis and Commentary
    Sections 1–5.. 11
    Sections 6–10....................................... 16
    Sections 11–14...................................... 19
    Sections 15–23...................................... 22
    Sections 24–27...................................... 27
    Sections 28–38...................................... 30
    Sections 39–41...................................... 35
    Sections 42–44...................................... 38
    Sections 45–47...................................... 40
    Sections 48–51...................................... 41
    Sections 52–54...................................... 44
    Sections 55–59...................................... 47

Addie Bundren and the
   Birth of Her Children 49

Darl and Addie Bundren:
   A General Interpretation 52

Notes on Main Characters
    Anse Bundren 58
    Cash 59
    Jewel 60
    Dewey Dell 61
    Vardaman... 61

Faulkner's Style and Imagery 62

Review Questions 65

Theme Topics 66

Selected Bibliography 67

As I Lay Dying Notes

LIFE AND BACKGROUND

Among Faulkner's total body of works, *As I Lay Dying* stands as a companion piece to *The Sound and the Fury,* the novel which was published the year preceding the publication of *As I Lay Dying.* The earlier novel is a criticism and condemnation of the so-called "aristocracy" of the South; the latter, a criticism and condemnation of the backwoods hill people who, through their ignorance, deny any value to life. Other similarities between these two novels are readily noticeable. A mother who affects the destiny of her children, levels of awareness presented through startling techniques, and characters who advocate a nihilistic philosophy are seen in both novels. Darl's searching questions into the meaning of life strongly suggest the disturbed personality of Quentin Compson (the son in *The Sound and the Fury*), and in a vaguer sense, Benjy's idiocy is again reflected in Vardaman.

William Faulkner (1897-1962) was born in New Albany, Mississippi, but his family soon moved to Oxford, Mississippi. The action of almost all of his novels takes place in and around Oxford, which he renames Jefferson, Mississippi. Faulkner, therefore, was very familiar with the type of person presented through the characters of the Bundrens. Even though Faulkner is a contemporary American, he is already considered one of the world's greatest novelists. In 1949, he was awarded the Nobel Prize for literature, the highest prize awarded to a writer.

Most of Faulkner's novels probe deeply into the mores and morals of the South. He was not hesitant to criticize any aspect of the South. This may seem surprising, since Faulkner came from a rather distinguished Mississippi family. His grandfather, Colonel William Culbert Falkner (the "u" was added to Faulkner's name by mistake when his first novel was published and he retained this spelling), came to Mississippi from South Carolina during the first part of the nineteenth century. The colonel appears in many of Faulkner's novels under the name of Colonel John Sartoris. Colonel William Falkner had a rather distinguished career as a soldier both in the Mexican War and the Civil War. During the Civil War, Falkner's hot temper caused him to be demoted from full colonel to lieutenant colonel.

After the war, Falkner was heavily involved in the problems of the reconstruction period. He killed several men during this time and became a rather notorious figure. He also built a railroad and ran for public office; he was finally killed by one of his rivals. During all of these involved activities, he took out time to write one of the nation's best sellers, *The White Rose of Memphis*, which appeared in 1880. He also wrote two other books but only his first was an outstanding success. The intervening members of the Falkner family are not quite so distinguished as was the great-grandfather.

With the publication of his third novel, *Sartoris*, Faulkner placed his novels in a mythological county which he called Yoknapatawpha County. The county seat was Jefferson, the town to which the Bundrens are carrying Addie to be buried. Most of the rest of Faulkner's novels take place in this county. Some of the characters in *As I Lay Dying* have already appeared in a preceding novel or will appear in a later work. The Tulls and the Armstids appear in several short stories and in a couple of other novels but not as main characters. Peabody appears in several places. The wild horse that Jewel possesses is the subject of one of Faulkner's most successful short novels, *Spotted Horses*.

Thus, one of Faulkner's great achievements is the creation of this imaginary county. He worked out his plan so carefully that we feel we know a character when he later appears in another work. With the publication of *Absalom, Absalom!* in 1936, Faulkner even drew a map of this county and showed the places where certain events took place.

In all of his work, Faulkner has used new techniques to express his views of man's position in the modern world. In his early works, Faulkner viewed with despair man's position in the universe. He saw man as a weak creature incapable of rising above his selfish needs. Later, Faulkner's view changed. In his more recent works, Faulkner sees man as potentially great or, as he expressed it in his Nobel Prize speech and in *A Fable,* "man will not merely endure; he will prevail." But in almost all of his novels, Faulkner penetrated deeply into the psychological motivations for man's actions and penetrated deeply into the dilemma in which modern man finds himself.

Of *As I Lay Dying,* Faulkner writes that he wrote it in six weeks while working on the night shift (from twelve midnight to six A.M.) in a heating plant. He would fire up the boilers, then using an overturned wheelbarrow, he would write until the boilers needed firing again. Of Faulkner's many achievements, this novel is one of his most popular.

STRUCTURE AND NARRATIVE TECHNIQUE

In its broadest terms, the structure evolves around the preparations for and the actual journey from the Bundren farm to a town forty miles away in order to bury Addie Bundren. During the journey, several difficulties are encountered. So, in one sense, the novel has a linear structure based upon the movement of the funeral procession traversing the forty miles from the Bundren farm to Jefferson. But the novel is also structured in such a way that the author has virtually removed himself from the story. He allows his characters to tell their own story. Accordingly, each of the fifty-nine sections is narrated by some character in the novel. Even though there are several important narrators who are not Bundrens, the largest number of the sections is presented by one or the other of the Bundrens.

By using a different narrator for each section, Faulkner accomplishes many things. First, he allows or forces the reader to participate in the story. Since Faulkner has removed himself from the story, that is, since he doesn't use a straight narrative technique to explain certain aspects, we must enter more directly into the story and determine for ourselves the exact nature of each relationship or the significance of any particular event.

Second, the technique allows us to know the inner thoughts of all the characters. We see into the mind of each character directly and must analyze what we find there. Faulkner, as author, has not told us anything about the characters — he has simply presented them and we must examine their inner thoughts and determine for ourselves what types of characters they are.

Third, we are able to see each event from multiple perspectives. For example, when the coffin is lost in the river, we have several narrations which allow us to see the same event from many different vantage points. For example, Darl gives his narration of the loss of the coffin; from Vardaman, we hear of his mother being a fish swimming in the river; from Cash, we hear that the coffin wasn't on a balance, and from Anse, we hear that this is just one more burden we must endure before he can get his false teeth.

Therefore, with the multiple narration of each event, we see that event from many angles and observe what type of emphasis each character puts on that event; by this technique, we learn more about the character. Thus, in general, the structure of the novel allows the reader to become a part of the narration by drawing him more intimately into the novel.

But Faulkner has also included some narrators who are not Bundrens. These narrators help to bring a touch of objectivity to the novel. Without the outside narrators, we might become too involved in the unusual Bundren world. Faulkner is therefore careful to include outside narrators so as to remind us that the Bundrens are not typical people. For example, if the story were confined solely to the Bundrens, then we might not realize that this dead body stinks so badly and that the Bundrens are violating all sense of decency by carting the body over the countryside. Thus, the outside narrators give us a touch of the real world by which we can measure our reactions to the Bundrens.

Therefore, if a central problem of the novel involved the reasons for Addie's request to be buried and why her family defy fire and water to fulfill it, then the structure of the novel forces the reader to solve these problems by analyzing each character.

LIST OF CHARACTER-NARRATORS

One of the difficulties most often encountered by the reader is the confusion caused by Faulkner's unusual and experimental narrative technique. Since Faulkner does not appear as the omniscient author but uses the thoughts of others to reveal the story, the following list of characters might aid the reader in readily comprehending the interrelationships among the various characters, who also serve as narrators.

Addie Bundren

The dying mother, who has ordered her coffin to be built under her window and who has extracted a promise from her family that they will take her to Jefferson to bury her.

Anse Bundren

Her bumbling and ineffectual husband, who is anxious to take Addie to Jefferson so he can get some false teeth.

Cash

Their oldest son, who is the carpenter and who builds the coffin for Addie. He is about twenty-nine.

Darl

The second son, about twenty-eight. He is the son most given to introspection and thought.

Jewel

The violent son, who owns the horse and who is ten years younger than Darl.

Dewey Dell

The sixteen-year-old, unmarried pregnant daughter who is trying to find a way to have an abortion.

Vardaman

The youngest son. His age is never given.

Vernon Tull

The helpful neighbor who has helped Anse so long that he can't quit now.

Cora

His wife, who spews forth self-righteous religious axioms.

Peabody

The town doctor, who weighs over two hundred pounds.

Samson

The neighbor where the Bundrens spend the first night of the journey.

Armstid

Another country farmer who helps the Bundrens during the journey.

Whitfield

The preacher who years ago had an affair with Addie and who conducts her funeral.

Moseley

The ethical druggist in a small town who is indignant at Dewey Dell's request that he help her with an abortion.

MacGowan

An unethical druggist's assistant who deceives Dewey Dell.

ANALYSIS AND COMMENTARY

SECTIONS 1-5

(NOTE: Faulkner did not number the sections, since he was interested in creating a continuous impression; therefore, the following attempt to divide the novel into sections and groups is made so as to facilitate critical commentary.)

Faulkner's technique throughout the novel is to present short individual sections in which some character gives his thoughts about the events which are taking place. Each section is an "interior monologue," that is, an attempt to reproduce what the character might be actually thinking. Therefore, if the character is in the presence of other people, often his thoughts will be interrupted by the conversation and often the character will record that conversation before continuing with his line of thinking.

In its largest view, the novel will concern itself with the death of Addie Bundren and the long arduous journey which the family undertakes in order to bury her in Jefferson, a town forty miles away. In these first parts, however, Faulkner is introducing some of his characters. The first section introduces the introspective Darl, who is the only son who is fully aware of all types of sensory images and impressions. Many of his sections will be characterized by his sensitive awareness of all the physical sensations around him. Through Darl, we come to feel the land and the people, and it is by him that most of the novel is narrated.

The first section also introduces the death and coffin theme. In only a matter of a few pages, it becomes clear that the older brother Cash is building his mother's coffin under her window so that she can inspect it. From Darl, we hear that Cash is a good carpenter and that their mother could not expect a better coffin than the one which Cash is building.

Darl's section also introduces another image which will re-appear throughout the novel. First, Darl is always aware of Jewel's eyes and particularly their wooden quality. Throughout almost all of Darl's sections, he will describe Jewel in wooden imagery and often associate Jewel with the wooden wagon. Later, when Darl and Jewel are earning the three dollars for the load of lumber, Darl tells of the death of Addie Bundren while Jewel is in a "wooden" setting.

Cora Tull's section is the first of many sections narrated by an "outsider." Faulkner apparently thought that his depiction of the Bundren family would gain more credence by having them viewed by neighbors, strangers, and other people. But he is not content merely to use these outside narrators to objectify the plot; he also creates vividly realizable characters.

For example, Cora is a delightful caricature of the country woman who spouts forth religious clichés. She is carefully deline-ated as a character because, as the novel progresses, we must have some outside narrator to rely upon who will give us varying views of the Bundren family. Not all of her observations are valid, but we must evaluate them in the light of what we know Cora to be as a character. For example, Cora's view of Dewey Dell as a blank person who stands indolently by her mother and fans her is picked up and repeated many times in later parts of the book. Also, Cora observes that even though Addie Bundren is dying, there is no sense of salvation or grace about her. Later, we will discover that Addie is a violent and somewhat nihilis-tic woman who rejects such words as "salvation" and "grace."

In Section 3, Faulkner is again setting up Darl as the perceptive person receptive to all types of detail. He describes with poetic imagery the simplest detail, such as taking a drink of water. The other narrators do not attempt to record their ideas in any type of poetic language. Furthermore, Darl is also highly perceptive when it comes to human evaluations and understanding behavior. For example, he understands his father's ineffectual behavior and knows that his father is incapable of a definite action.

Darl's perceptive ability is further suggested in his visualizing the scene between Jewel and the horse. This technique is employed many times in the novel when Darl will frequently narrate a scene or an event even though he is not present at the event. This technique or this ability of Darl's has led some critics to suggest that this is an indication of Darl's possible madness.

The description of Jewel's relation to the horse is quite significant, since Jewel's love for his horse and his relationship with this horse is one of the central ideas in the novel. For example, in the scene which Darl visualizes for us, Jewel acts with violence toward his horse, but beneath the violence there is a sense of deep devotion to the animal. This particular dichotomy characterizes Jewel as a person who feels violently and can only express himself—even love—through acts or images of violence. Consequently, the violence of this short scene with the horse leads directly into Jewel's only narration.

Since Jewel is one of the most significant characters in the novel, it is at first puzzling that he narrates only one section in the entire book. We see Jewel from every other perspective; that is, we see him from Darl's viewpoint, from Cash's, and so forth, but this is our only chance to get into Jewel's own mind and see his personal thoughts.

Essentially, this section reveals Jewel's very deep but inexpressible love for his mother. He is unable to express his love in any way except in symbols of violence, as was displayed in the last section by the manner in which he violently caressed his horse. Consequently, it is often in symbols or images of violence that we observe Jewel, and this violence is later correlated with his birth, since he was, according to Addie, conceived in violence. Furthermore, later on, Darl will also taunt Jewel by saying that Jewel's mother is a horse.

Jewel's love for his mother is expressed in terms of standing on a high hill and throwing rocks down the hill at anyone who would intrude upon the privacy of his love for his mother. This violent image suggests the violence with which he does love his mother—a violence which will come to an end only after she is buried and Darl is sent to the insane asylum.

Later in the novel, it is Jewel who violently saves Addie from both water and fire. Section 4 serves to illustrate Jewel's need for violence, and only through violence can he express his deep-founded and deep-rooted love for Addie. Thus, since Jewel can express himself only through acts of violence, we have only one section narrated by him. All of the other views of Jewel are through some other narrator's eyes.

Jewel offers one humorous insight into the character of Cash, prompted by the fact that Cash, the most literal-minded of the children, is actually building the coffin under Addie's window. Jewel recalls that when Cash was young, his mother asked him to bring her some fertilizer from the barnyard and he took the bread pan and brought it back filled with dung. This illustrated Cash's literal-mindedness and prepares us for some of his later sections where we see him functioning only on a very literal level.

With the above incident, Faulkner introduces us to one of the interesting techniques in the novel which involves the juxtaposition of something that is extremely serious—the building of the coffin—with something that is inordinately comic—collecting dung in a bread pan. The juxtaposition illustrates how Jewel is trying to express his deep emotional love for his mother and his resentment that Cash is building the coffin under her window, as though he were anxious for her to die so that he can see what a good job he has done. Yet to express his idea, Jewel resorts to a comic scene involving Cash as a young boy bringing dung in a bread pan.

Throughout the entire novel, we will have many comic aspects juxtaposed with a potentially tragic scene. The structure of the novel depends heavily upon this tragic-comic combination, and it is sometimes difficult to analyze our response to such scenes.

As Darl confronts his father about the need of hauling the load of lumber and the practicality of securing the three dollars, we realize that Darl has a strong practical side to his nature and furthermore knows how to go about accomplishing such a task. Later, it will be Darl who will be sensible enough to prevent the fight in Jefferson between Jewel and the town man. The reader should take these facts into account when trying to determine the degree of sanity which Darl possesses.

However, one could also view Darl's desire to deliver the lumber as another method of tantalizing Jewel, of taking Jewel away from his dying mother. Darl is certainly aware that Jewel is unable to face any type of reality where his mother is concerned. Jewel refuses to believe that she is dying and even refuses to say the word "coffin." Darl is acute enough to notice this reluctance and explains it by saying that Jewel doesn't know how to express his love and speaks with harshness so as to cover up the fact that he can't say the word coffin.

Since Jewel can express his love only violently, Anse then completely misunderstands him. Anse thinks that Jewel has no love for his mother and no respect for her. But, as Darl points out, it is because Jewel loves her so strongly and so violently that he acts as he does. Darl's perception is further indicated in the manner in which he judges his father. He mentions that once when Anse was young he was sick "from working in the sun" and now believes that if he ever sweats he will die. But Darl knows that Anse uses this excuse to cover up for his laziness.

SECTIONS 6-10

In these next sections Faulkner continues presenting his various narrators and characters in the novel. By the time the reader has finished Cora's second narration, he should be aware that Faulkner is creating a magnificent picture of the backwoods, self-righteous, superficial woman. It is ironic that with these qualifications Faulkner will allow her to make some basic and true observations of the other characters. For example, in Cora's section we hear for the first time that Darl is somewhat different from the other Bundrens. This basic idea will become central to the novel, since in the final scenes Darl will be declared insane and will be sent to the asylum outside of Jackson, Mississippi.

In this section Cora also mentions that Darl is the one whom people consider to be strange or queer. But at the same time she makes the observation that he is the only one who can get things done without causing too much dissension. Darl's strangeness, of course, will later be equated with his insanity, yet at the same time Darl is the only Bundren who can accomplish a simple task in a straightforward manner.

Cora makes another observation which is important because it concerns the relationship between Darl and Addie Bundren. Cora comments that the truest understanding and love exists between Darl and his mother. Consequently, from this one neighbor we have the view that there is a special type of relationship between Darl and Addie and yet at the same time Cora also recognizes that Addie is more partial to Jewel.

Cora's final observation is that Addie Bundren even in death is still filled with excessive pride. But throughout all of these observations, as noted previously, the reader must be ready to respond to them only in terms of the individual section. That is to say, Cora is not the most intelligent or the most impartial witness in the novel. Therefore we cannot put too much reliance on her comments, but at the same time we must be prepared to react as if they might be the truth.

Section 7 of the novel introduces the daughter, Dewey Dell, who will ultimately turn out to be one of Faulkner's great comic creations. And at the same time she will be seen to be an exceptionally vicious person in her feelings toward Darl. The tension which develops between Dewey Dell and her brother Darl results from Dewey Dell's pregnancy, which Darl seems to know about.

We are never to know definitely how Darl has come to discover that Dewey Dell is pregnant, but on account of his taunting her about her condition, Dewey Dell develops an intense hatred for her brother, and this hatred will later cause her to attack him violently. We are of course led to believe that Darl is the type who can project himself into the personality of another person and automatically know what that other person is thinking. It is perhaps through such a mysterious procedure that Darl learns of Dewey Dell's pregnancy.

An example of Faulkner's superb humor is seen in the reasoning behind Dewey Dell's seduction. Faulkner, along with other great writers like Chaucer, is never afraid to enter into the most elemental, bawdy, or earthy type of humor in depicting his characters. In this section we see Dewey Dell trying to disclaim all responsibility for her seduction and her later pregnancy by a strange, perverted, deterministic reasoning process — one that assures her that she will definitely be seduced by Lafe. Her reasoning is almost a type of fatalism on her part. We can later assume that her reasoning process is so basic and so simple that she cannot think silently. Therefore, it is possible that during the above reasoning process she has been talking aloud. Consequently, Lafe could have heard her reflections and put cotton into her sack so as to make sure that it is full by the time she reaches the end of the cotton row; then it follows that she must have sex with him. This action on Lafe's part is a definite pun on Faulkner's part; that is, Lafe fills Dewey Dell's cotton sack with cotton so that he might fill her womb sack.

The section narrated by the neighbor, Vernon Tull, introduces us to one of the more objective and reliable narrators. Tull is a simple, basic, and honest person who has none of the religious fervor or prejudice of his wife, and who records events as they appear to him without any comment about them. Accordingly, we can basically accept Tull's narration as objective because he does not concern himself with side comments. He simply renders the scene as he sees that particular scene.

In Tull's section we are also introduced to Vardaman and the fish which he has just caught, both of which will become very important in later chapters. Likewise Tull also makes an observation about the weather, thinking that it is soon going to rain. This rain will hinder the trip that the Bundrens must make toward Jefferson.

In an earlier section we had seen Anse Bundren say, as though he were a completely self-sufficient and independent person, that he will never be beholden to any person. In Tull's section we receive an outside view of how independent Anse really is. Tull comments that he has helped Anse for so much of their lives that it would be difficult for him to stop helping him now. Consequently, Tull's statement conforms to Darl's analysis of his father, and we are beginning to realize that Anse is a totally ineffectual individual who needs someone to take care of him. The ineffectuality of Anse, of course, leads us directly into the next section, which is narrated by Anse himself.

Anse Bundren's main occupation is sitting on the porch and watching the road, which he resents because he had to pay taxes in order to build the road. But even the smallest task is a great hardship for Anse. When he tries to explain something his thoughts become totally confused. Any effort to accomplish something requires a great deal of deliberation and he finds as many excuses as possible to avoid doing any work at all.

The arrival of the doctor is also told first through Anse's point of view. This is significant because Anse begrudges the money that he has to pay the doctor. His only interest is in getting his false teeth, and if he has to pay the doctor because of Addie's sickness he will not be able to get them. We also realize that Anse would never have called the doctor on his own volition.

Anse's desire to get his teeth will later play a strong role in motivating his promise to take Addie to Jefferson to bury her.

Vardaman and the fish image reappear even in Anse's section, an image which will continue until Vardaman confuses his mother with the dead fish.

The tenth section, narrated by Darl, seems to totally disregard time, but the reader should remember that this section occurs while Jewel and Darl are away from the house. And yet during the section he taunts Dewey Dell as though she were present also. In other words, Darl is able to visualize and recreate scenes from the past and present them as though they were in the present.

Darl seems to like to taunt both Dewey Dell and Jewel. These taunts may reveal a very perceptive sensibility; for example, we hear him accuse Dewey Dell of wishing her mother dead so that she, Dewey Dell, can get to town to have an abortion. So Darl can both instinctively know that Dewel Dell is pregnant and can also know that Dewey Dell is anxious to get to town. Later we will see that Dewey Dell is the person who violently insists that Anse keep his promise to take Addie to Jefferson.

Darl's delight in taunting, teasing, or antagonizing both Dewey Dell and Jewel may possibly be accounted for by the fact that Darl senses the deep-founded love between Jewel and his mother, so he seems to take either some perverse or jealous pleasure in taunting Jewel.

SECTIONS 11-14

In the total body of Faulkner's writings, Dr. Peabody will appear in several works and he always retains the same characteristics. That is, he is the overweight, friendly humanitarian, the person who grasps the very nature and essence of a person's character, but who is yet willing to devote his time to his patients' welfare. Indicative of this is the fact that he has on his account books almost $50,000 in bad debts. It is a Faulknerian technique to use the same character in many novels.

Consequently, when Dr. Peabody appears as one of the narrators in this work, the reader of all of Faulkner's novels knows immediately that this is an intelligent and reliable witness to the Bundrens' qualities. He is included so that the reader can have this outside objective view of the Bundren family, and Dr. Peabody is the most objective commentator in the novel. For example, his view is essentially an accurate description of Anse Bundren.

Dr. Peabody also makes several other observations which are quite accurate. His description of Addie suggests that she is a woman who has lived terribly alone and that she is simply exhausted from having lived for so long with Anse Bundren. In fact, the doctor ironically or sarcastically suggests that it is good Anse didn't call him too soon because he might have been able to save Addie Bundren and prolong her unbearable life for additional years with such a person as Anse Bundren.

The death of Addie Bundren as narrated by Darl presents many questions for some critics. For example, why does Faulkner choose to have Darl render or narrate the death scene when he is not even present? This technique emphasizes Faulkner's method of narration and his characterization of Darl. The intuitive and perceptive abilities of Darl allow him to visualize a scene even though he might be miles away from it. That is, Darl knows exactly how his father, his brother, and Dewey Dell, and other members of the family will react to the death scene even though he is not present at the scene. We must assume, therefore, that Darl in going for the load of lumber must have known that his mother was going to die or else that he has some exceptional perceptive ability which allows him to sense her death even though he is not present. This ability will also contribute to the suggestion that Darl is, if not mad, at least different from the other Bundrens.

If the reader was not aware of it before, he must now realize that Cash is building his mother's coffin under her window so that she can watch and see that he is building her a good one. The comic aspect of this situation is almost lost in the pathos of

Addie's death. But then the entire section is a combination of that which is tragic and that which is comic. For example, the selfishness of Anse Bundren is caught in one simple phrase, which he utters immediately upon learning that his wife is dead. There is no mourning, there is no thought other than for his own selfishness concerned with obtaining his new teeth so that he can eat the food that God intended him to eat.

The section narrated by Vardaman, Section 13, is the first direct view we have inside Vardaman's mind. The youngest son can find no way to express his grief for his mother's death and therefore he at first begins to blame the doctor, since this man is a stranger to him. Then he begins to wonder about the fish that he caught that afternoon at the pond. He remembers watching the fish die and then he begins to wonder about his mother's death. Gradually in later sections, these two deaths will become confused and interchangeable, but this is the first hint of this forthcoming change. Vardaman's confused thinking is expressed in terms of him striking at Dr. Peabody's horse in an attempt to express his grief over the death of his mother. This confusion of how to express his grief is later reflected in his confusing his mother with the dead fish.

Dewey Dell's narration presents her again as a person almost incapable of reason. She is trying to worry but she is also incapable of worrying. She is almost incapable of any emotion except that of animal desire. Consequently, images often connected with her are those of the bovine animals of the farmyard. The cows are described in the same imagery with which Dewey Dell is described. In her passage she even says she would like to worry but she cannot think long enough in order to worry about anything.

Like her mother, Dewey Dell yearns for something to "violate" her aloneness, and she also yearns for some act of violence, but she is incapable of understanding these two emotions.

In this section the imagery of Vardaman and his fish is also repeated and gradually the fish, in general literary terms, a symbol of regeneration, is reversed here to suggest the symbol of death and disintegration.

Whereas in the last section we found that Vardaman had been feeding Dr. Peabody's team, now in this section we find out that Dr. Peabody's team has run away. Ironically, Cash, the oldest son, wants Vardaman to go after the team because he thinks that Vardaman can catch and handle the team. This refers essentially to an old folktale that a person who is slightly mentally retarded is able to communicate with and manage animals better than the normal person. And later on in the novel it is somewhat obvious that Vardaman is either retarded or else that he is much younger than the implied 12-14 years.

SECTIONS 15-23

Section 15, narrated by Vardaman, begins to juxtapose various animals and their breathing. Vardaman's recollection of his rabbits, his dead fish, and his being once trapped in a crib occurs simultaneously with his inability to accept his mother's death as a physical reality. The concept of death leaves him confused as to the nature of reality and thus causes some of his vague and strange statements and acts.

All of these remembrances are Faulkner's preparations for presenting Vardaman's confused mind. Through these associations and others, Vardaman is gradually confusing his dead mother with the dead fish that he caught that afternoon. But already Faulkner has been preparing the reader for the shocking revelation. By this point in the novel the reader should begin to note that even among the bizarre Bundrens, Vardaman is a little different from the others.

Even though this section is narrated by Vardaman, another motif is introduced. We have previously seen that Anse is anxious to get to Jefferson so as to get his new teeth. Dewey Dell is anxious to get there so as to get an abortion. Vardaman also has his selfish motives as illustrated by his desire to see a toy train in a store window. These personal considerations will ultimately become more important than the burial of Addie Bundren and the promise that she extracted from them to bury her in Jefferson.

In Section 16, narrated by Tull, Vardaman is still associating the death of the fish with the death of his mother. Both memories evoke other memories of when he was not able to breathe because he was in a confined place. Therefore when Vardaman comes home, he opens the window so that Addie can breathe.

Apparently his grief is of the sort that is suffocating, or, in other words, he associates the idea of suffocation with the idea that his mother is now suffocating in a coffin. Consequently, when they finally put Addie in the coffin, Vardaman's various associations between breathing, the dead fish, his dead mother, and so forth, cause him to think of his mother as a fish that is unable to breathe in the small coffin. Therefore he bores holes through the coffin so that his mother can breathe, but in doing so he also bores holes in his mother's face.

This scene embraces then both the comic in a gothic and grotesque way, and the tragic in a pathetic way. Vardaman cannot express his grief and he is so neglected as a child that in trying to help his mother and in trying to alleviate his own sense of grief, he unintentionally mutilates the dead body of his own mother. Perhaps part of the greatness of the novel is that the reader does not know how to respond to such a scene, whether the response should be one of horrified tragedy over the ultimate and final result, or whether one should respond with a grotesque comic view of the entire episode.

The fact that Faulkner allows Vernon Tull to narrate this bizarre section adds to the confusion of our response. The reason that Tull narrates this section is that he is such a dull person, therefore emphasizing the contrast between Tull as a dull and objective narrator and the bizarre aspect of the scene that he narrates. These two elements then complement one another; that is, the scene is so bizarre that it gains in effect by being reported in a quiet, unemotional, and objective manner.

In the midst of the scene we have one observation that is seemingly unimportant, but the reader should hold it in abeyance. That is, Tull comments that Darl thinks too much. This at least indicates that Darl is an introspective person concerned with the intricacies of the mind, whereas the other Bundrens simply accept things as they come.

Darl's narration in Section 17 again conforms with Faulkner's technique of allowing Darl to narrate a scene when he is not present at the scene. Again this shows Darl's perceptive qualities. He can envision his father making comments about Addie Bundren's death, and he can picture Anse saying that he does not begrudge the work that Addie has caused him. But at the same time, we know that Anse is doing nothing.

Furthermore, Darl also realizes that Cash is more concerned about building a good coffin than he is about his mother's death. This indicates Darl's understanding of Cash's character, that is, that Cash is a person who can only concentrate upon one thing. As long as he has the coffin to build, Cash cannot concern himself with grief or mourning for his mother. Once the coffin is completed, then Cash will be able to turn his mind to other thoughts.

At the end of Darl's narration we note that he enters into a rather intricate thought process. The two characters in the novel who are concerned with their relationships to others, that is Darl and Vardaman, both try to establish the exact relationship that they have with other members of the family, and Darl, more so than Vardaman, is concerned with trying to determine the exact nature of his own personal existence. Consequently we will find Darl constantly questioning himself in terms of his own existence.

Both Section 18 and Section 19 — the first narrated by Cash, the second by Vardaman — are called *tours de force*. Cash has so far been depicted as a rather literal-minded person who could concentrate only on one thing at a time. Here, in the first section to be narrated by Cash, he presents in numbers 1 through 13 the exact technique of building a coffin. This humorous, comical, and untypical narrative technique, then, reinforces the interpretation of Cash as being literal-minded.

In Cash's narration there is no mention of his mother's death. All of his energy, his thoughts, have gone into the making of the coffin, and the coffin is of supreme importance. Now that the coffin is completed Cash can turn his mind to something else, but this something else must also occupy his entire thought process.

The Vardaman section, the shortest section in the novel, having only five words, is also a *tour de force*. Faulkner has been leading up to this statement by Vardaman's many associations of his mother with the fish. All of the preceding actions and imagery connected with Vardaman have been leading up to this statement, but it nevertheless comes as a surprise.

Again the reader is involved with another question, that is, is this section the height of comedy or is it extremely pathetic? Most people would agree with the combined qualities of both the comic and the pathetic. But how is one to respond to a comic assertion by a confused young boy that his dead mother is a fish?

Vardaman's attack on Cora and his running away are additional suggestions that he does not understand the idea of his mother's death and knows no conventional way in which to express the grief that he does not understand. His confusion will continue until after Addie is buried.

Tull's narration also conveys some important factual information: (1) We find out that the bridge is washed out, necessitating a longer trip down the river that will require extra time. (2) We find out that Addie has been in the coffin three days before Darl and Jewel get back with the wagon. And in a hot Mississippi July rainy spell, this is a long time to have a dead body above ground. (3) We receive more facts about the perfection with which the coffin was built.

Other than the factual information, we also receive certain impressions. Armstid, a new character introduced in this section, suggests that the Bundrens would do much better if they would bury Addie Bundren in the nearest town. This prepares us for the fact that the body will indeed be in the advanced stages of decay before they can possibly reach Jefferson and the burial ground that Addie has requested.

Perhaps the most grotesque bit of information conveyed in this section is Tull's narration of how Vardaman bored a hole into the coffin and in doing so actually bored some holes into his mother's face. Again, as in Section 16, the reader must evaluate his own response to such an episode, which contains both the potentially comic and the potentially tragic. Under any circumstances it is one of the most ironic scenes in the novel, since this bizarre episode is narrated by the dull and unimaginative Tull.

It is also comic that Cash's precision will let him give the exact distance that he fell when he broke his leg. That Cash has broken a leg previously is important to know, since later on when he breaks the same leg trying to rescue the coffin, Anse will say that it is lucky that he broke the same leg that had previously been broken. But also Cash's giving the exact measurement of the distance that he fell when he broke his leg emphasizes that Cash exists in a world of well regulated fact, and that he is concerned with how well the coffin is made according to balance, measurement, and weight.

In Section 21, narrated by Darl, three important thematic ideas are employed: (1) Jewel as wooden, (2) Jewel's mother as a horse, and (3) Darl without a mother. Darl's taunt that Jewel's mother is a horse indicates that Jewel devotes all the love he possesses for his mother on the horse. The horse has become a type of mother symbol, but only Darl is perceptive enough to be aware of this. However, Darl does not realize that when Jewel was conceived that Addie thought of Jewel as being conceived in violence, so therefore the symbol of the horse, a violent and untamed horse, as the symbol of the mother conforms with the circumstances surrounding the birth of Jewel and also answers the question of why Jewel himself expresses his love in terms of violence.

Jewel is constantly depicted by Darl and to a lesser degree by other characters as having a wooden appearance. In this section alone he is described both as "wooden-backed" and "wooden-faced." This wooden imagery contrasts ironically with Jewel's violent and agitated motions.

Darl's realization that he cannot love his mother because he has no mother is also a perceptive realization that will become clear later. When we come to Addie's section, we find that Addie rejected Darl before he was born because she realized that a birth could not "violate" her aloneness. And since she did reject Darl, this is represented in Darl's sense of rejection by his mother. This thought will be developed much more fully in later sections but is introduced here.

Section 22, narrated by Cash, emphasizes again that Cash is concerned only with one thing, the immediate construction of the coffin. In terms of the later action of the novel, Cash's emphasis that the coffin will not ride on a balance is partly justified since we can assume that the loss of the coffin in the river is due in part to the fact that it was not riding on a balance.

Even though this is a short section and the person to whom Cash is talking is not identified, we can easily assume that the person is Jewel because of the violence of his language and his predilection for action rather than talk and analysis. The same type of violent language is in fact picked up in the next section, Section 23, which is narrated by Darl and which records Jewel's furious and desperate movements which serve to replace any type of verbal expression of grief. Jewel's actions, then, are seen in terms of despair and fury and his only comments are curse words, indicating once again that he can find no adequate way of expressing his grief for his mother's death.

SECTIONS 24-27

The beginning of the journey is announced by Vardaman, who seems to have already forgotten the grief for his mother and instead has simply substituted in his mind that his mother is a fish. With the confusion of his mother with the fish, Vardaman begins to examine the other relationships and begins to wonder why Darl calls Jewel's mother a horse.

The height of comic irony is seen when Anse thinks it is not respectable for Cash and Dewey Dell to use the trip to town for purposes other than attending to Addie's funeral, that is, Cash is carrying his toolbox and will stop off on his way back to begin work on a barn, and Dewey Dell is carrying Cora Tull's cake, which she will try to sell for Cora. (Actually, Dewey Dell is carrying her Sunday clothes—not the cake.) Anse, however, is going to town to get new teeth, and as we find out in the last section, to pick up a new wife as soon as Addie is buried. Therefore his comment about Cash and Dewey Dell is a good example of comic irony.

In Section 25, narrated by Darl, the imagery of Jewel as being wooden-backed is again emphasized. And again this wooden imagery is juxtaposed against the violence of his actions and furious movements.

In Section 26, narrated by Anse, we once again have Anse offering a type of evaluation and criticism of his children, but we know from previous encounters with Anse that he is totally incapable of understanding any member of the family. For example, he is annoyed that Jewel brings the horse on the trip with him. He feels that out of respect for his dead mother that Jewel should not ride the horse. But as has been noted earlier, Jewel uses the horse as a symbol in replacement for his love for his mother. Having the horse with him then, is Jewel's way of expressing his love, and Anse totally fails to understand the connection and can only think that it is disrespectful, when in reality it is Jewel's acknowledgment of his grief and love. Anse's view is ironic because, later on, it is only by selling the horse that they can continue on the journey.

There have been several hints that people talk about Darl or look upon him as different. Anse seems to be aware that Darl

is also different and views his constant laughter as a sign of
Darl's strangeness.

An important question then to the total interpretation of the
novel is, Why does Darl laugh? We, the readers, have become
very familiar with Darl as the sensitive and perceptive narrator.
We must then try to create for ourselves the same scene that
Darl observes. This scene would involve a pregnant, barefoot
girl in a wagon, an ineffectual father murmuring clichés, a young
and perhaps retarded brother, a half-crippled brother, the coffin
of his dead mother, and then suddenly over the hill comes the
other brother riding a half-wild horse.

Consequently, it can be maintained that this is a rather
ridiculous situation and that Darl laughs because he is intelligent
and perceptive enough to recognize the absurdity of the entire
situation. Or then perhaps Darl laughs because he begins to
understand why Addie wanted to be buried in Jefferson, a reason
which does not become clear to the reader until a much later
section. And finally, perhaps this is an indication of a certain
degree of madness on Darl's part. Perhaps, then, Faulkner is
preparing us for the later scene when Darl will be violently
attacked, tied up, and sent off to the insane asylum.

Whatever interpretation or however the reader interprets
this scene must ultimately depend on how he views various
aspects of the novel, and he must then utilize his entire reactions
to every theme so as to arrive at a consistent view of the motivating factors which cause Darl to laugh. In the next section
narrated by Darl, note that whenever Darl takes over the narration, we get a fuller and more comprehensive view of the procession in vivid and dramatic images.

Now even Cash notes that the body will soon be decaying
and giving off odors. And the reader should also remember that
Addie has been dead a full three days and it is in Mississippi
in July. Darl has already made the observation earlier, but
here he contents himself with suggesting that it would not be

30

wise to speak of the decaying body to Jewel, who reacts so
violently to any mention of his dead mother.

The central image of this section is that of the wagon toiling
slowly along while Jewel, on his contrasting spotted horse, is
circling the wagon with violent and furious motions. Symbolically, Jewel seems to be encircling his mother while at the same
time riding the horse which is a symbol of the replacement of
his mother. Again Darl refers to Jewel in terms of wooden imagery, which contrasts to the violence of the actions performed
by Jewel and relates him then to the wooden wagon slowly pull-
ing the wooden coffin.

SECTIONS 28-38

These sections present one of the more crucial and significant episodes of the novel, that is, the arrival at the bridge and
the loss of the coffin while attempting to ford the high waters.
The introduction to the washed-out bridge is presented from
Anse's viewpoint and again presents Anse as a man who does
nothing but who feels that he must endure untold burdens for
the sake of others. Actually, however, as the end of the section
indicates, Anse's only concern now is with getting his new teeth.

We hear more of the Bundrens by the introduction of a new
objective commentator. This is Samson, a neighboring farmer,
and with him Faulkner takes us away from the Bundren world
for a while. At this point in the novel we need to see the normal,
or average or typical, reactions so as to be able to evaluate the
absurdity of the Bundrens' actions.

When Samson first sees the Bundrens, we hear him assume
that the Bundrens are taking a holiday, now that they have buried Mrs. Bundren. The irony here, of course, is that the average
person would assume that a woman dead for four days would not
be carted about the country in the back end of a wagon. Consequently by this one assumption, the absurdity of the Bundrens'
actions is further indicated.

Later, Samson expresses the idea that the best way to respect a dead woman is to get her into the ground as quickly as possible. Samson's section, then, adds a note of objectivity by reminding the reader of the proper perspective and of the normal reactions of the average person toward the dead. And since the body is beginning to decay so rapidly, and since we see it from the outside narrator's point of view, we are prepared later on for Darl's drastic actions in trying to give his mother a decent and respectable funeral when he burns the barn.

What Samson does not understand is that Anse is using the promise to his wife as an excuse to get to Jefferson for his false teeth. But Dewey Dell is even more insistent than Anse about getting to Jefferson. It is she who reminds him of his promise. But then in actuality Dewey Dell is not interested in her mother or in fulfilling the promise, but only in getting to Jefferson so that she can have an abortion.

It is somewhat comic that Anse consistently asserts his independence and will not become indebted to anyone while at the same time he is constantly accepting help from someone.

In Section 30 Dewey Dell narrates a short scene; mainly her narration is one of impressions. Her scenes are essentially illogical because, as Dewey Dell herself says, she is incapable of thinking, of remembering, or tying things together. She responds only on an elemental level. In remembering the fish that Vardaman caught and stuck the knife into, she juxtaposes this previous scene with an imaginative scene of violence in which she stabs Darl. This image of violence foreshadows her later attack on Darl at the end of the novel and should be seen as her subconscious desire to punish Darl because he knows of her pregnancy. Dewey Dell herself seems to be unaware of the significance of the buzzards, and they seem to gain significance for her only in the fact that Darl constantly watches them.

Sections 31 and 33 are both narrated by Tull, but these sections are interrupted by the narration in which Darl recounts for us the story of Jewel's obtaining the horse. In Tull's narration we note once again Anse's complete helplessness when confronted with some obstacle, in this instance, the washed-out bridge. The irony here is, of course, that Anse cannot perform any action and he can only mouth generalizations, hoping that someone will soon come to his rescue.

Tull's observation of Darl is interesting in view of our final analysis of Darl. Tull makes the remark that Darl has always been considered somewhat strange, and in Tull's view what Darl says is not as strange as is the manner in which Darl looks at a person. This conforms with our general view of Darl. We have seen that Darl has the ability to penetrate into another person's thoughts or subconscious, especially Dewey Dell's and Jewel's.

In Darl's section, we see how dedicated Jewel can be when confronted with the task of earning money to purchase a horse. This dedication should be juxtaposed to his love for his mother. His desperate efforts to earn money for the horse are partly the reason why he loves it so dearly, and this also accounts for part of the pathos when he has to sell it to help complete the journey to Jefferson.

In this section it becomes almost certain that Jewel knows that Anse is not his father. Jewel has a pronounced antagonism toward Anse, as seen when Jewel promises that he will never allow his horse to eat any of Anse's food.

The entire section concerning the purchase of the horse leads us deeper into the relationship existing among the various Bundrens. For once we see Darl and Cash both as having some type of almost brotherly affection for Jewel. But more important Faulkner also gives us an inside view of Addie, who is somewhat partial toward Jewel. We see her doing things for Jewel in secret, even though she has always maintained that deceit was one of the worst sins.

Tull's continuation of his narration leads to one minor problem concerning time in the novel. That is, earlier the Bundrens had passed by the Tulls and gone and spent the night with the Samsons, and then in these sections we hear that Tull followed them immediately after they left the house. We can account for this only by saying that again Faulkner is not presenting the story in strict chronological order. That is, these sections by Tull can be considered a jump back in time. Yet Samson in his section has also suggested that the bridge is out. The important thing, though, is that Tull is totally unable to determine why the Bundrens must cross the water.

As noted previously, whenever a significant event occurs, the reader should be aware that it is Darl who narrates this event. Thus, he is also responsible for the main narration about the losing of the coffin. The narration itself is in language that is impressionistic, musical, and imagistic, rather than a straightforward narrative. However, we do gain a sense of the immediacy of the situation.

In the attempt to cross the river, we again have the basic attributes of Cash and Jewel demonstrated. Jewel is impetuous and has no logical plan for the crossing. Instead, he simply must be doing something—must be performing some action. He cannot tolerate the slow process of thinking or working out some plan and his impatience is partly responsible for losing the coffin. In contrast to Jewel, Cash is slow, deliberate, and calculating. He likes to think over every possibility before he begins anything, and it is Cash who wishes to secure the coffin better and to have a rope on the other side as a brace against the current. Yet because Jewel cannot stand the delay, they begin the crossing before they are certain of its success.

In the next narration by Vardaman, we have another view of essentially the same event. And in the following section, Tull again gives us still another view of the same event. These three sections taken together are an excellent illustration of the narrative technique Faulkner uses. That is, he narrates the same event from several perspectives so that the reader can gain a fuller understanding of the event.

Earlier Vardaman had confused his mother with the fish he caught on the day she died. This scene, then, combines the height of comic irony with tragic pathos as the pathetic Vardaman associates his mother's body, now apparently bobbing and floating in the river, with a fish. Faulkner does not narrate this directly; therefore, the reader must imaginatively reconstruct the scene in his own mind in order to grasp the grotesque pathos of this entire section.

Tull's narration is apparently some time later in time, since he is telling his wife Cora what happened. Throughout the entire episode at the river Faulkner never mentions what Anse is doing. Whenever there is some emergency or some action that must be performed, Anse is most often rendered totally incapable. For example, during the confusion caused by the overturned wagon in which each character is desperately involved in some type of furious activity, Anse is completely absent from the scene. Imaginatively, the reader can envision Anse as a mere bystander shaking his head and muttering one of his platitudes.

Faulkner again utilizes Darl to narrate another aspect of the ill-fated crossing. And again we should notice that Anse can merely stand ineffectually by and bemoan his predicament, but he does nothing to rectify it. And when he says that he does not begrudge Addie the effort, he is actually thinking only about his teeth.

It is typical of Anse that he thinks it is lucky Cash broke the same leg, when in reality this is the worst possible thing that could have happened. But Cash himself does not even think about his leg. Cash, even in the midst of the pain of his broken leg, is more concerned about the reason that the coffin was lost. Ironically, this concern again suggests that Cash cannot become involved in more than one thought at one time. Since the opening of the novel his entire attention has been focused upon the mechanics of the coffin itself, and since he is so proud of his handicraft, it is ironically fitting that he will be compelled to ride on top of it.

SECTIONS 39-41

These next three sections function as a type of interlude. It takes the reader away from the funeral procession for a few moments and we go briefly back into time. In a sense, Cora's section functions as an introduction to Addie's section, which is then followed by Whitfield's section.

One of Faulkner's greatnesses is the care which he lavishes on his minor characters. They stand out as separate entities along with their function of illuminating one of the major characters. Here Cora, a minor character, receives that attention which causes her to become one of the memorable minor characters. Faulkner has perfectly captured the religious fanatic who spouts forth superficial religious axioms. But in reality she possesses a great deal of pride in being or thinking that she is humble. For example, we can evaluate Cora's comments by the fact that she thinks that Brother Whitfield is a godly man if ever any man is godly. And yet we later learn that the preacher Whitfield is the father of Jewel as a result of his adultery with Addie.

Cora's comments about Addie function as an introduction to Addie Bundren's only section. It is from Cora, the religious fanatic, that we hear Addie's statement that Jewel will be her salvation, that he will save her from the water and from the fire. Her statement carries with it a religious tone, and the prophecy is later fulfilled. That is, we have already seen Jewel saving Addie from the river and later he will save her from the burning barn. Furthermore, it is only because Jewel sells his horse, the symbol of his love for his mother, that they are able to continue the funeral procession.

Cora's comments about Addie, then, introduce us to her as a person who is not religious, as a person who has not devoted her life to God or to the church. We are then prepared to meet a woman who has embraced a rather nihilistic philosophy.

Halfway through the novel and halfway through the long journey to bury Addie, Faulkner inserts the only section narrated by her. Since her section comes in the midst of the funeral procession, it serves to remind the reader that she was a real person and not just some dead, stinking object in the box.

Addie seemed to hate the children that she taught, and so she would beat them to make them aware of her. This seems to be one of the driving forces in her life, that is, to make people aware of her presence. Thus one may say that when she failed to make her family aware of her during her life she extracted a promise from them so that they would be aware of her at least during the arduous funeral march.

We cannot maintain that Addie wanted to be buried close to her father or to her family in Jefferson because she reveals in this section that her father taught her a rather nihilistic philosophy. Her actions conform to her father's view that life is no more than a preparation for death. Furthermore, it is suggested many times that she hated her father for having sired her. Consequently there is no indication that Addie extracted the promise merely so that she could lie in death next to her family.

Since Anse is incapable of giving us any background information, we have to rely upon Addie's account of their courtship. We see that Addie married Anse because there was nothing else to do. She was tired of the children, tired of teaching school, and she says that when Anse came along she simply accepted him without any thought. There is no implication of love but simply a marriage of convenience.

The circumstances surrounding the birth of each child in some way affects the personality of the child. For example, Addie says that she gave birth to her oldest son, Cash, so that he could "violate" her aloneness and make her feel that someone is aware of her. Thus throughout Cash's life he has existed as a person who can concentrate only upon one thing. After she had Cash she realized that even children cannot "violate" her aloneness; therefore she did not want any more children. When she discovered that she did have Darl she detested Anse and began to reject Darl himself. Consequently throughout his life,

Darl has felt as though he has had no mother and that he is the unwanted and rejected son.

Addie then thought that if she could engage in some type of violence, her "aloneness" and her isolation could be violated. When she met the Preacher Whitfield, she felt that if she could have an affair with a man whose garments were sanctified then the sin would be "more utter and terrible." While hoping for some type of violence, she conceived Jewel, who is seen as a person whose acts are constantly presented in terms of violence. Dewey Dell was conceived in order to negate Jewel, and then she had Vardaman so as to give Anse a child in place of Cash, whom she considers her own. Consequently Dewey Dell seems to possess no love for her mother and functions more as a robot. And Vardaman himself is somewhat retarded or at least somewhat strange.

Addie's general view of life is nihilistic and this perhaps is reflected also in her children. As noted above, Addie can function only in terms of violence. She searches out some act of violence that will penetrate her sense of aloneness. Essentially, Addie seems to be a rather destructive personality, and as a mother she is unable to love her children openly. Instead she infects them in some ways with her terrible view of life. Only in secret can she really give of herself and offer love to Jewel, but she hates herself for this also.

Addie's view of words is that they are unclear. Essentially, she seems to imply that people substitute meaningless words for significant actions, and thus, with this view, she would detest Anse because all Anse can do is murmur platitudes. We have seen that he is incapable of performing any task, however small or trivial it might be, thus rendering him useless except for his words. On the other hand, Cash never uses words and speaks only after some fact or deed is accomplished. Jewel similarly expresses his love not in words but in acts of violence. And Darl, the one who most relies on words, is the one most rejected by Addie and ends up being sent to the insane asylum.

Consequently Addie, who feels that she has been deceived by words, decides to get her revenge on Anse by extracting a promise — which is of course only words — to take her back to Jefferson, and this would be her revenge because then Anse would have to perform some action rather than relying on words.

Immediately after hearing from Addie that she had had an affair with a preacher, we then encounter the preacher himself. Furthermore we had heard that Addie went to Whitfield thinking to experience a violent and overpowering reaction from the preacher. But this section shows that Whitfield is also only words. He is going to let his intention to confess replace the actual confession, emphasizing Addie's evaluation that even Whitfield was only ineffectual words.

SECTIONS 42-44

With the resumption of the journey, Darl's narrations become much more intricate and involved. The intricacy of his narration might be Faulkner's way of preparing us for Darl's later problems with alleged insanity. For example in Section 42, the technique employed is that the parts in italics refer to Jewel and the normal print refers to the actions of the other Bundrens. Darl's mind is not focusing on one incident but is fluctuating between two or more incidents.

Again in this section we are in the presence of a mixture of the comic and tragic. Cash's leg apparently hurts so badly that he is only semiconscious and vomits when they move him. But his vomiting makes Anse think that maybe he got a kick in the stomach, whereas Cash is suffering from the constant movement of his broken leg. Likewise, the safest place they can put him is on top of the wet coffin. But even though Addie doesn't smell as bad at this moment because of the dunking in the water, in the final analysis this soaking will cause the body to deteriorate even more rapidly. Thus, in total, the scene is almost fantastic or absurd and possesses elements of the pathetic, the humorous, the grotesque and the tragic.

Equally pathetic is the brutal treatment that Cash has to undergo. However, all through these episodes Cash never utters a word of complaint and simply accepts that which he cannot escape.

Throughout these sections the selfishness and hypocrisy of Anse are further revealed. The reader must keep in mind that during the episodes Anse himself has money which he has saved for his new false teeth, although he claims that he sacrificed the money to buy the team. Moreover, he steals from his own children.

These sections also indicate something of Addie's prophecy. It is fulfilled only because Jewel allows his horse to be sold so that the journey can continue. For Jewel to sacrifice his horse indicates the extent of his inexpressible love for his mother.

While Darl's thought processes are becoming more intricate, Vardaman's thought processes become somewhat more confused. He is trying in these sections to determine the family relationships to one another.

Vardaman has never been able to accept his mother's death. It does not conform to any sense of reality that he has thus far encountered. His thinking, while confused, is an effort to bring divergent facts into a logical whole. He thinks of his mother as a fish and of Jewel's mother as a horse, and yet he knows that he and Jewel are brothers. Thus his confusion is a type of method in madness: he makes valid conclusions while working with false premises.

The dominant image throughout these sections is that of the buzzards, which have increased in number as the journey progressed. These buzzards then function as a horrible reminder of the inhuman desecration of Addie Bundren's dead body.

Finally it is revealed that Cash must suffer so tremendously because Anse does not want to be "beholden" to the Armstids by leaving Cash there in a bed. We assume that as long as it is someone else who is suffering, Anse doesn't mind too much.

SECTIONS 45-47

The section which is narrated by Moseley is given as an ultimate contrast to the later section narrated by the Jefferson druggist, MacGowan. Each druggist then functions as a comment upon the other. This section also plays an important function in that it gives the reader the outside view which is again needed. For too long we have remained with the Bundren family. Suddenly it is made clear to us that Addie is just a dead rotting body which is now eight days old in a hot Mississippi July sun.

Through the indignant responses of the Mottson sheriff and the druggist, we gain an impartial view of the Bundrens which helps us to prepare for Darl's reaction in the forthcoming sections. And finally that the Bundrens are buying concrete so as to repair Cash's leg reminds us of the incompetence of the entire Bundren family, and our opinion is confirmed by the sheriff's horror at the idea of the Bundrens undertaking such a task. The sheriff's outside, objective view forces us to maintain a distance from the actions of the Bundrens and aids us in analyzing them objectively.

Section 46, narrated by Darl, captures that strange essence which flavors this entire part of the novel. While it is never stated directly, we know that Anse is going to put the home made concrete cast on Cash because he has already bought the cement — not to use the cement would be a foolish waste. Ironically, Cash is much worse off with the cast than he would have been without it.

Vardaman then takes over the narration and still tries to determine the exact relationships among the family, but his thought process is interrupted by his concern with the buzzards.

His concern though is, in reality, only out of curiosity to see where the buzzards stay at night. This concern will allow him to be present when Darl sets fire to the barn.

SECTIONS 48-51

In Section 39 we heard Addie say that Jewel will be her salvation, that is, he will save her "from the water and from the fire." Prior to her narration we had the water episode in which Addie's coffin and body were rescued by Jewel. During these sections we have the fire episode in which Jewel will risk his own life in order to save Addie from the burning barn.

Section 48, narrated by Darl, shows how Darl continues to taunt Jewel by questioning who he is. Jewel obviously knows that Darl is referring to the fact that he does not have a father and that he was the result of Addie's adulterous affair with the Preacher Whitfield. These taunts partially justify Jewel's later attack upon Darl, and particularly the violence with which Jewel later attacks Darl. Of equal importance though is why does Darl continue with these taunts? Is he in reality being only malicious and spiteful, or could it possibly be that he is trying to force Jewel to come to an understanding of his relationship with the family? There is a strong argument in favor of the latter, since Darl has constantly been concerned with his own relationship to the family. Jewel has seemingly functioned outside the family, and by his taunts Darl hopes to force Jewel to recognize his involvement and hopes to force him to act as a member of the family rather than as an isolated individual.

This section also prepares us for the later action of removing the cast from Cash's leg. We observe here that Cash's foot is beginning to swell and that he is in pain, owing to the improvised cast.

In the early part of this section, Darl tells Vardaman that he heard his mother asking to be hidden from the sight of man. This is one of the motivating reasons behind Darl's decision to burn the barn. It can be assumed that Darl saw through the ridiculousness and absurdity of the entire procession. It can also be assumed that, since Darl can see into the thoughts of others, he knows that everyone is going to Jefferson for selfish reasons. Therefore, he wants to thwart their selfish motives, and at the same time give his mother a respectable cremation. Or one may say that he wants to give her a cleansing through fire and thus remove the odorous absurdity in the coffin that is offending the entire countryside.

Faulkner has prepared the reader for this section. He has very carefully shown us Darl's ability to penetrate into the thoughts and motivations of others, and he has also shown us the selfish motivations of the other members of the family. Thus, Darl, who sincerely loves his mother, feels that he is benefiting her by giving her this cleansing cremation. But the reader should remember that it is this action by which the other Bundrens declare Darl to be insane. Therefore, we should watch his remaining actions to judge whether or not he is actually insane.

The reader should also step back from the novel and realize the consequence of Darl's act in terms of the rural community in which he lives. To burn a barn during the time just prior to harvesting, to endanger the lives of the animals in that barn, and to destroy farm property could easily be viewed by rural people as an act of insanity. In earlier stories Faulkner had even used the concept of barn-burning as one of the most dangerous types of crimes to be committed on a farm.

For these people, therefore, in spite of all justifications for Darl's act, the mere fact that he has destroyed property so essential to the management of a farm would automatically cause many people to view him as being partially insane. Thus it is up to the individual reader to determine the exact nature of Darl's sanity and insanity. The final justification for Darl's act is rather ironic and it is represented by the repeated refrain in this section of the strong smell of the body. We must remember that Addie has now been dead for over eight days and the stench must be overwhelming.

The implication in this section is that Vardaman saw Darl setting the barn on fire. We must project that Dewey Dell's motivations here are to get Darl declared insane, and then Darl would have no chance to tell Anse that she is pregnant. This reasoning, of course, is rather ironic, since it will be impossible for her to conceal her pregnancy for many more months. But she still hopes to get the abortion in Jefferson.

The actual narration of the barn-burning is again given by Darl. The contrast between Darl's sensitive and rather quiet narration and Jewel's furious and determined actions is important. Jewel's entire personality is captured in the desperate flights in and out the barn. It is only through violent actions that Jewel is able to express himself. In contrast, it is only through words that Darl is most able to express himself. Therefore Darl's narrating of this section captures the essence of Jewel's violent personality.

As noted above, Addie had told Cora that Jewel would be her salvation. Thus this section fulfills the prophecy that Addie made by showing how Jewel saves her from the fire. We should also be aware of Jewel's actions because he first gives all of his attention to the mules. He knows that unless the mules are rescued it will be impossible to get the body to town. He has no intention of leaving the body to burn with the barn, but he also knows that the mules would not leave the barn if the fire were too fierce. Thus the mules which were bought with his horse, the symbol of his love for his mother, were first rescued so as to assure the completion of the journey, and only then, at great danger to himself, does he return to the barn to rescue his mother's body.

This section also shows that Dewey Dell is terribly concerned over the fate of Jewel. We may project that her concern is partially based on the fact that she knows Jewel hates Darl also and will join her in turning against Darl later.

The combination of pathos and humor in this scene is handled masterfully. We laugh at the ignorance and at the absurd actions of these Bundrens, but at the same time, we respond with opposite emotions since a human being, however comic, is undergoing intense pain. Thus, we cannot view these scenes as entirely comic since, according to the Aristotelian definition, comedy cannot consist of any scene where physical pain is inflicted upon a person. Consequently, we must classify these scenes as a combination of pathos and humor.

Again, Darl's sanity or insanity must be viewed in terms of how other people react to him. After all, it was Anse Bundren who declared him insane, but as has been noted, Anse is not a reliable judge of character. From outside viewpoints such as that of Gillespie, we realize that the uninvolved person looks to Darl to perform the rational action and is surprised to discover that Darl did not prevent Anse from applying the cement. This idea is then doubly ironic when the Bundrens send Darl to the insane asylum.

Vardaman's view of Darl is that he thinks Darl is upset because Addie almost got burned up. Instead, Darl feels the pathos of continuing this absurd trip and is crying because his mother has not been given a cleansing funeral. In all the previous outside views, the other people have expressed the idea that the best way to honor a woman dead so long is to get her in the ground as soon as possible. This is exactly what Darl was trying to do — give his mother a decent and honorable funeral.

SECTIONS 52-54

In Section 52 Darl notices the effect of the arduous journey on all of the family. But even though he is exhausted, he is still in control of the situation, as is illustrated in the central episode in this section — that is, the attempted fight between Jewel and the white man. The reader should note that whereas Anse merely stands around saying "fore God," it is only Darl who is rational enough to take over and prevent a serious fight between Jewel and the white man. In fact, Darl handles the episode with perfect composure and equanimity. Without Darl we can project that the entire procession would have been interrupted and perhaps much confusion created by Jewel's impetuous action.

The question is, what motivates Jewel's actions in this section? It is obvious that Jewel is now aware of the tremendous stench coming from the coffin. But his love for his mother will not tolerate other people's commenting on the horrible stench. Jewel's violence then continues as long as his mother is above ground.

For the first time in the novel, Cash rises above his mundane thought processes in order to contemplate the problems of sanity vs. insanity. The experiences which Cash has undergone during the course of the journey force him to consider problems abstractly and not in terms of specific numbers. Consequently, after recognizing that Darl's actions are logically correct and that what Darl did was indeed the proper behavior, he must be compelled some time in the future to view the recent actions of the Bundrens as bizarre and incoherent. For such a man as Anse Bundren, it is much easier to declare his son insane than it would be to pay for a barn.

While admitting that Darl's actions are correct in an abstract or theoretical manner, Cash is still confronted with another dilemma. That is, Cash knows that a barn is of inestimable value to a farmer; therefore, the destruction of a farmer's barn must be the act of a man who is insane. Thus, Cash can justify the intent of the act but not the actual act.

But as for Cash, who believes so strongly in the sense of property, he cannot understand Darl's willingness to destroy someone's property. That Darl attempted to destroy Mr. Gillespie's property, he thinks, is cause enough to allow Darl to be put in the insane asylum.

The reference in Section 53 to Mrs. Bundren's house is confusing. Actually, Cash is narrating this section at a time when he knows that this lady will be Mrs. Bundren in a few hours.

Dewey Dell's attack on Darl shows the degree of antipathy she felt for him. Darl has taunted her for so long that Dewey Dell now releases all of her pent-up feelings against him. She does these things because Darl has taunted her for so long about her pregnancy and now she feels that she is getting her revenge and also removing her sense of torment, or at least her tormentor.

Darl thought that Cash would have told him that the family meant to send him to the asylum because Darl knows (as does Cash know) that there has never been any sense of antipathy or conflict between him and Cash. On the contrary, there was a sense of closeness. Darl apparently realizes that even Cash is unable to see the logic and necessity for his (Darl's) past actions. Darl's laughter is provoked because he can perceive the "metaphysical absurdity" of the situation while his brother, Cash, can only respond to the immediate act.

Why does Darl laugh? We have seen how Darl was able to see into the motivations of others, and now we must assume that he sees into all the motivations and understands how and why the others are afraid of him. He also understands that he is being declared insane so that Anse won't have to pay for the barn. These realizations leave Darl no alternative except to laugh or else actually lose his last bit of rationality. Thus at the end, the reader is once again reminded of the doubt surrounding Darl's supposed insanity.

Section 54, narrated by Dr. Peabody, returns us to the objective, outside view of the Bundren world. We have been so closely involved in the actions of the Bundrens that we need, at this point, an objective narrator to remind us of the total absurdity of the preceding actions. For example, the treatment that Darl receives, by analogy, is seen to be as absurd as putting the concrete on Cash's leg. Thus, we find that the outside narrator views Darl's insanity with skepticism. We are almost prepared to assert that the behavior of the Bundrens as seen by the outside narrator is more incomprehensible (or insane) than was the action of Darl.

SECTIONS 55-59

Section 55 is one of the most humorous sections in the book. It is filled with earthy and bawdy humor. It shows the small-town rascal taking advantage of the country girl, a classically humorous situation in American folktales.

The reader should make the contrast here with the druggist from Mottson who became indignant with Dewey Dell. The earlier druggist is seen to be very ethical and offers Dewey Dell some good advice. But this second person (who is actually not a druggist) merely uses Dewey Dell for his own pleasure.

By the end of this section, we know that all of Dewey Dell's efforts (including her attack on Darl) are of no avail; she is still pregnant and will remain so.

Section 56 is another view of the same event narrated in the preceding section. After Dewey Dell emerges from her seduction, she knows that it is not going to work. Her comment (that it won't work), which is repeated as a sort of refrain, is essentially comic in that she approached her seduction in the same way as the cow crosses the square, just clopping on the street.

Section 57 gives the casual reader the impression that perhaps Darl is insane. But the careful reader has seen Darl's intricate reasoning powers earlier in the book. As Darl looks at his predicament, he laughs to himself about the absurdity of it all. One might say that his position is so absurd that he must laugh or else really lose his sense of balance.

The reader must also recreate in his mind the exact nature of the scene that Darl sees, and then the reader will realize that this scene is innately comic. Perhaps here Darl laughs because he realizes how fortunate he is to escape from this bizarre Bundren world.

In the last two sections, Faulkner is showing the reader the type of world or family which Darl is escaping from. In this section, we see that while Anse has been murmuring platitudes about how a man should respect a dead woman, he has actually been preparing to marry the "duck-shaped woman." And the reader, who knows the Bundrens now, would have to agree that a sensitive person such as Darl is indeed better off anywhere rather than with the Bundrens.

ADDIE BUNDREN AND THE BIRTH
OF HER CHILDREN

Addie Bundren's attitude at the time of the birth of each of her children is reflected in the personality and actions of the child. Addie herself was born an isolated and lonely soul, openly unloved by her family and rather strongly affected by the nihilistic philosophy of her father, who had taught her that the reason for living was no more than an extended preparation for death. Addie felt that during her whole life she had been neglected, and when she married Anse, she hoped that through the violence of birth that she could achieve an awareness of life and force her presence upon others. She is dreadfully afraid of aloneness and thus through committing or participating in some type of violence, she feels less alone. Thus when she knew that she was pregnant, she felt that at last her aloneness had been penetrated, especially through the forthcoming childbirth.

Cash had penetrated into her aloneness, and had thereby given meaning to her life. Cash then is the firstborn and is at peace with the world and earth as he works on one level of consciousness, performing one task at a time, slow and calculating. He was conceived as an act of violence, and his life reflects this in that he can express himself only through some type of action, such as the building of the coffin. Thus, there was no conflict between Addie and Cash.

But soon after Cash's birth, Addie realized that words are not connected with violence and are useless. Thus she decides to close herself to Anse, who represents only the ineffectuality of words. Only through violence, and not through words, can Addie feel that she is living. But then, as she came to this conclusion, she discovered that she had Darl. Thus Addie felt that somehow she had been tricked by Anse's words and because she had been tricked, she could never accept Darl. The very fact that the words had tricked her was proof enough that Darl could never help violate her aloneness.

And it is ironic that Darl is the one son who continually inquires into the intricacies and awareness of life. Thus in later life, Darl, through his intricate thought-process, was able to sense that he was the unwanted and "motherless" child. In view of Addie's rejection of words and her subsequent rejection of Darl, it is ironic that Darl became the one character who depended the most on the value of words.

For ten years, Addie closed herself to Anse. She said that Anse was dead even though he did not know that he was dead. But after ten years, Addie met Whitfield, the preacher, and she saw in him the symbol of the violence which she had been seeking because the "garment which he had exchanged for sin was sanctified." Addie believed that Jewel had been conceived in violence, and he therefore became her natural choice for salvation. But both the love and the salvation have to be products of violence. In Jewel's life, this violence is displayed through the love and violent treatment of his horse and the salvation is seen through his rescuing Addie's body from the river and the burning barn. Thus Jewel, who was born as a result of Addie's desire for violence, responds to all events with violent and impetuous actions, and he seldom says a word except some violent oath or curse.

After the affair with Whitfield, Addie began to prepare for her own death. She admits that she gave birth to Dewey Dell "to negative Jewel" and to Vardaman to "replace the child I robbed him of." Thus Dewey Dell, born only as a replacement for, or to negate, Jewel, is the child who most resembles Anse. She moves in an orbit of egoism, seeing each action only as it immediately affects her. And as with Anse, she cares only for herself, and uses any amount of deceit to get her own way.

And finally Vardaman, born, not from love, but to replace another child, reflects this by replacing his dead mother with a dead fish.

Thus the actions surrounding the birth of each child are reflected in his behavior throughout the novel. Faulkner's purpose was to show how the Bundrens are unable to establish satisfactory relationships within the family. Addie Bundren is egocentric, interested more in forcing an awareness of herself on others than she is in caring for the needs of her children. But Addie possesses the sadistic strength to force her violence upon the lives of her children. Her own egocentricity is, in one way or another, reflected in her children.

Vardaman's repeated statements that he is not "anything" reflects Addie's opinion that people are nothing when they are not "violating." Dewey Dell is nothing because "I am alone." And Dewey Dell also shows Addie's egoism as she acts only for her own selfish satisfaction. Addie's need for violence is reflected in Jewel, and her desire to let the act replace the word is seen in Cash, who speaks only after some act is definitely performed or completed.

Darl, it will be remembered, was born unwanted and at a time when Addie came to the realization that she had been tricked by words. Darl, therefore, has Addie's awareness of the complexities of life, but as the rejected son, he rejects Addie's nihilistic philosophy of violence and destruction. Using his awareness, however, he seeks to achieve a sympathy and understanding with the family. This attempt lands him in the insane asylum.

Thus the novel shows the family perishing as a result of a negative philosophy which infects or destroys the whole family as either a meaningful unit or as individuals capable of arriving at some understanding of life. The novel has depicted a family where the mother substituted negative values for love. And all of this can be seen in the epiphany scenes surrounding the birth of each child.

52

DARL AND ADDIE BUNDREN:
A GENERAL INTERPRETATION*

One key to a basic interpretation lies in the relationship between the psychological motives for the journey to Jefferson and the attitude of the Bundrens toward Darl. The first problem is concerned not merely with the fulfillment of the promise made to dying Addie, but with both the reasons why Addie demands this promise and the reasons why her family defy fire and water to fulfill it.

Addie had always seen herself as being completely alone in the world. She sensed that her own father did not love her. Thus when he died, she had no kin left. When Anse came along, she was glad to escape from the loneliness of teaching school. She dismisses her courtship with the curt words: "So I took Anse." Faulkner mentions no love or emotional understanding, just an acceptance — and maybe not even an acceptance but a conditioning for death. For Addie all living had to be some type of preparation for death. She had felt alone so much during her life that her great desire was to make other people aware of her presence. And she felt that only through violence could she achieve her aims. She also felt that words are useless, and she soon comes to realize that Anse (and later preacher Whitfield) are just words.

Thus Addie built her life around violence. But she had failed to make her presence felt by other people. She finally came to the full realization that during her life she had also been only words; after death, she was determined that it should be otherwise. Consequently, feeling that she would attain reality only when she imposed herself upon the consciousness of others, she made them promise to carry her to Jefferson, forty miles away, to bury her.

*The following is a condensation of the article "The Individual and the Family: Faulkner's As I Lay Dying," by James L. Roberts which appeared in *The Arizona Quarterly*, XVI, No. 1 (Spring, 1960), 26-38, and is reprinted with permission.

The first problem of this novel is to understand why Addie makes Anse promise to carry her back to Jefferson. We discover early in the novel that she bore no love for her own family and, eventually, even hated her own father when she discovered the need for violence in order to achieve awareness. Thus we must assume that Addie made one more desperate effort to force an awareness of herself on her family. This difficult and arduous journey was to be her revenge on Anse, who had been only words, who had failed to help her achieve awareness, and who had never violated her aloneness. Addie even acknowledges that part of her revenge would be that Anse "would never know I was taking revenge." Thus Addie's request to be buried in Jefferson was made essentially for selfish reasons, in a last effort to prove that she was not just useless words.

For all Addie's efforts to force an awareness of herself upon the consciousness of her family, she partly fails. Anse is quite content to carry out the promise — not because it is a promise and not because of his respect or awe for the dead. People of the Bundren type have seen death too often to view it as other than an event in everyday life. But, "God's will be done ... now I can get them teeth" is the extent of Anse's feelings. He lives only in the world of ineffectual words. Without the outside help of Samson, Armstid, Tull, and Gillespie, Anse would never have made it to Jefferson. Even then he has to steal from his own children in order to replace destroyed equipment.

However, Anse makes sure that he does not steal so much that there won't be more left to steal — for his teeth — when he gets to Jefferson. He must also rely on other people to get the grave dug, since he didn't bring a spade and refuses to buy one. When the water incident and the fire occur, Anse is always the bystander, commenting: "Was there ere a such unfortunate man," thinking that all these events are just more crosses he must bear before he can get his teeth. The irony of the situation is that Anse is constantly indebted to others but refuses to recognize his obligation and excuses himself by his oft-repeated comment: "I aint beholden."

With Dewey Dell, Vardaman, and Cash, Addie's efforts to force an awareness of herself on her family again fail. Because of her pregnancy, Dewey Dell is interested only in getting to the druggist in town. Vardaman lives also in a vegetative world, and his is also a world of confusion. He is almost oblivious of his mother's decaying body and looks forward only to seeing the toy train in the store window. Cash sees only one action at a time; therefore, his only concern is with each immediate action. Only upon Jewel and Darl is Addie's presence deeply felt, and ironically these are the two that she least wished to affect.

After the relationship between Addie and the rest of her family has been established, the next problem lies in Darl's relationship to the Bundren family, and especially their attitudes toward him. Darl is always elusive, complicated, thought-provoking, poetic in stream-of-consciousness observations, and especially observant of details. It is through Darl's eyes and observations that the reader gets a full perspective of the other characters.

Darl is the only character in the book who lives on several, interchangeable levels of consciousness. As a result of this perceptiveness, Darl is able to understand the feelings of others. Perceiving the relations between Jewel and Addie, he taunts Jewel about not having a father; and this taunt stems from Darl's realization that, because of the circumstances of his own birth, he has no mother. Darl is able to comprehend Jewel's inexpressible love for Addie and realizes that the emotions Jewel projects toward his horse substitute for his feelings toward his mother — hence, the accusation that Jewel's mother is a horse.

Not only does Darl understand Jewel's feelings for Addie, but he also realizes that Jewel is the "cross" that Addie bears. Consequently, Darl's descriptions or observations of Jewel are full of symbolic, wooden imagery.[1] Darl has penetrated Jewel's

[1]A few descriptions of Jewel as seen by Darl are as follows: "his pale eyes are like wood set into his wooden face," "eyes like pale wood," "his eyes like pale wooden eyes," "He sits...wooden backed," "Wooden backed, wooden faced," "Jewel sits on his horse like they both are made out of wood." For a further example see especially the description of Jewel against the background of a cross as Darl announces Addie's death. But there seems to be more to this than just wood for the cross. This wooden imagery also sets up an interesting contrast between Jewel's actions and his appearance. All of his actions are violent and impetuous, in contrast to his quiet, wooden look. During the early part of the

inner consciousness and sees the motives behind each of Jewel's actions. The tension mounts steadily between Darl and Jewel as Darl projects himself into the consciousness of Jewel and knows instinctively each of Jewel's motivations, and yet refuses to act. The tension suddenly increases after Jewel sells his horse and it culminates when, at the end, Jewel violently attacks Darl.

Darl's relationship with Dewey is similar to that with Jewel, but on a different level. Again, Darl has been able to project himself into another character's consciousness and senses all the implications concerning Dewey Dell's pregnancy. Her first comment to Darl is: "Are you going to tell Pa are you going to kill him [Lafe]?" But Darl again refuses to take any definite action; as a result, tension mounts steadily between Darl and Dewey Dell until she attacks Darl even more violently than does Jewel.

There is, however, no conflict between Darl and Cash, or between Darl and Vardaman. Darl is the only one who is able to project himself into the vegetative world of Vardaman, but no conflict arises, since Darl lives on a level far above that of either Cash or Vardaman. Darl and Cash are the only ones who feel a close kinship to one another. This comes mainly from Cash, who thinks that, after all, Darl was probably right in trying to burn the barn but that it should have been he (Cash) who performed the action. But Cash's reasoning is not intricate enough to reach any definite conclusions, since he lives only in the world of one-level actions.

As we progress through the novel, it becomes increasingly evident that Darl is the key figure to the solution of the complex interrelationships of characters. Darl's importance appears not only in his complex thought processes and his ability to perceive and sense everything, but also in the fact that most of the important action is presented through his eyes. Before leaving with the wagon to earn three dollars, Darl projects himself into the character of Addie. He later senses and tells of Addie's death in beautiful, heightened, poetic language.

---

journey, Jewel keeps encircling the slow-moving wagon with his horse, attempting, even after Addie's death, to achieve some status or awareness.

It is through Darl that the reader learns of the loading of the coffin, of Jewel's purchasing of the horse, of the loss of the coffin, of the recovery of the tools from the water, and of the burning of the barn. It is even Darl who prevents Jewel from becoming involved in a fight with one of the Jefferson townsmen. It is evident, therefore, that Faulkner wrote into the character of Darl a key to the Bundren family. Darl is portrayed as the sane and sensible individual pitted against a world of backwoods, confused, violent, and shiftless Bundrens.

As the journey with Addie's rapidly decaying and odorous body progresses, the animosity between Darl and Jewel, and between Darl and Dewey Dell, heightens swiftly and rapidly approaches a climax. Jewel becomes more and more antagonistic after he is forced to sell his horse—the living symbol of Addie, on which he had lavished his love and violence. As the tension mounts, Darl's perceptive ability becomes keener and more sensitive. It is Darl, and Darl only, who senses the futility of the whole ridiculous procession. In the beginning of the journey, seeing it in its absurd perspective, he is forced to laugh. Then as the body gradually gives off its odors, it is Darl who first senses this new absurdity, and it is Darl who first perceives the buzzards hovering overhead in all their horrible significance.

As the odors become stronger, as the buzzards increase in number, and as the journey becomes a ridiculous farce, Darl—sensitive, perceptive, and intelligent—realizes that something must be done to put an end to this grave injustice to his mother. Just before Darl sets fire to the barn, he senses the presence and desires of his mother: "She's talking to God.... She wants Him to hide her away from the sight of man ... so she can lay down her life ... we must let her be quiet." Thus Darl decides to end the futility and injustice by giving Addie a cleansing escape from the sight of man through cremation.

The barn burned, but Addie, still odorous as ever, was, in spite of Darl, saved by Jewel, in fulfillment of her earlier prophecy. This one act, mature and intelligent, performed by Darl, was the basis on which the Bundren family decided to send him to Jackson's insane asylum. There was never an actual question of whether Darl was insane or not: that had nothing to do with the decision. But as Cash put it: "It was either send him to Jackson, or have Gillespie [the owner of the barn] sue us." Cash realized that what Darl attempted to do was the right thing, but still, the Bundrens must call him crazy or pay for the barn, and it is much easier to declare Darl insane. Of course, Darl has always been considered queer by the other people in the novel, but this is because he is superior, and in being superior, he is different, and therefore, in their minds, queer.

Anse and Cash therefore declare Darl crazy for financial reasons; Jewel accepts it violently and anxiously out of the heightened enmity between them. And Dewey Dell, responsible for Gillespie's knowing that Darl burned the barn, is the one most pleased in disposing of Darl, thereby insuring the secrecy of her pregnancy.

Thus, Darl's supposed insanity is imposed upon him and a close reading of the novel suggests that Darl did not go insane. A study of Faulkner's methods in his other novels indicates that if Darl had gone insane the reader would have been made aware of his regression toward insanity. In the "Darl" passage immediately following the barn-burning, it is only Darl who is intelligent and sane enough to prevent Jewel from getting into a fight. As Jewel prepares to attack the town observer, Darl handles the situation with perfect sanity, composure, and equanimity.

Faulkner presents several objective views of Darl which create at least a doubt as to the validity of sending him to the insane asylum. Dr. Peabody looks upon the act of sending Darl to Jackson as a blundering episode typical of the acts of Anse. He compares the foolishness of this act with the foolishness of Anse's putting concrete on Cash's leg. Likewise, Gillespie, another objective commentator outside the Bundren world, looks to Darl as the only sensible Bundren capable of rational actions.

If Darl became insane, it is necessary to regard that as an instantaneous stroke of insanity; but this was not the case. What probably did occur, in that moment of clear and instant illumination when he began to laugh, was a complete comprehension of the absurd situation through which the family had just passed, and a thorough perception of the animosity between him and the others. This realization left him only one thing to do — to laugh loud and long at the ignorance of the Bundrens from whom he is escaping.

In his last passage, perhaps for a moment he even doubts his own sanity. He has never lived in a sane world, but only in the insane and incomprehensible Bundren world. When he refers to himself in the third person, he is merely reflecting to himself that he knows now what others have been thinking about him. He understands now all their hatred and envy of his superiority. A Darl Bundren in an insane asylum is in a much better position than an Anse Bundren in the outside world.

One of the great ironies of the book, consequently, comes from the fact that Darl, the only person capable of reaching an awareness of the complexities of life, is sent to the insane asylum while the rest of the Bundrens, who should probably be locked up, roam freely.

NOTES ON MAIN CHARACTERS

ANSE BUNDREN

Once when he was very young, Anse got sick from too much heat. Ever since then he tells people that if he sweats he will die. Therefore, he uses this as an excuse for not having to do any work. Instead, he sits on the porch uttering platitudes and thinking every time something happens, "Was there ere such an unfortunate man." Even when he makes an effort to help, as when Tull and Cash are finishing the coffin, he is so bumbling that he actually is more of a hindrance than a help, and he is sent back to the house so as to be out of the way.

Anse is the extreme hypocrite. He seems quite content to carry out the promise to Addie — not because it is a promise, and not because of his respect for his dead wife, but in his words, "God's will be done...now I can get them teeth." This is the extent of Anse's feelings. Thus he uses Addie's death to accomplish his own selfish motives. Furthermore, in order to fulfill his own aims, he will steal money from Cash while Cash lies unconscious with a broken leg, he will force Jewel to sell his horse, and he will forcibly take Dewey Dell's money. But he will not lift a finger to help anyone else.

But Anse is also a comic figure. He is so ineffectual and so bumbling that he is almost dismissed as an individual. When the water incident and the fire occur, Anse is always the bystander, thinking that all these events are just more crosses he must bear before he can get his teeth. But he always generously forgives Addie for the trouble she is causing: "I don't [won't] begrudge her...." The irony of the situation is that Anse is constantly indebted to others, but refuses to recognize his obligation and excuses himself by his oft-repeated comment: "I aint beholden."

CASH

Cash is the oldest son. He is the one Addie refers to when she says that she robbed Anse of one son. Cash was born at a time when his mother had just discovered that words are meaningless and that only through acts can man achieve an awareness of life. Thus, Cash seldom speaks in the novel and usually only after some action is performed. Furthermore, he seems to be concerned with only one act at a time. Thus he was the natural choice for the building of the coffin because he, like Addie, knows that the finished product is more important than the words expressed about it. And as he builds, he does not seem to be aware that his mother is actually dying—all his energies are concentrated upon the building of the coffin. His first section comes after he has the coffin almost completed, and this section simply enumerates the thirteen steps or reasons why and how he built the coffin.

Like Addie, Cash seems to know that words are useless. And when he breaks his leg a second time, he tries to protest that he doesn't want the cement on his leg, but again the words are useless and he simply resigns himself to the torture. He does not even bother to formulate words enough to express his tremendous suffering.

And when Darl is sent off to the insane asylum, Cash seems to be somewhat justified in his view toward words. He says that "aint none of us pure crazy and aint none of us pure sane until the balance of us talks him that-a-way." The act itself that Darl performed seems to Cash to be right; therefore, it was the talking about the act that convinced people that Darl was insane.

Therefore Cash reflects Addie's views about the uselessness of words and sees only one action at a time, and his main concern is with each immediate action.

JEWEL

Jewel seems to have the most violent nature of all the Bundrens. But actually, Jewel is not a Bundren, since his father was the preacher Whitfield. Jewel was conceived at a time when Addie was searching for some violent act which would give to her a sense of awareness. Her relations with the preacher Whitfield were to her symbolically more violent because his garments were sanctified.

Jewel has only one section to narrate. And in this section we see Jewel expressing his love in the most terrible images and thoughts. We see his deep-rooted, violent, but inexpressible love for Addie. Thus since Jewel is unable to express his love for his mother, he substitutes all of his love for the horse. Thus, later we get from Darl the accusation that Jewel's mother is a horse.

We eventually learn that Jewel is the "cross" that Addie bears and that he is to be her salvation. But Jewel is never able to act upon the level of either conscious or unconscious thought; his is a world of words and emotions translated into actions without the intercession of thoughts. In fulfillment of Addie's prophecy, it is Jewel who saves her from the water and the fire, and he is her salvation, since he sells his horse in order to complete the journey.

DEWEY DELL

Dewey Dell, who was born to negate another child, approaches life negatively—that is, she refuses to assume any responsibility for her pregnancy or for her mother's funeral. Because of her pregnancy, she is interested only in getting to the druggist in town. When something interrupts the journey, it is Dewey Dell who reminds Anse of his promise to bury Addie in Jefferson. But all the time, Dewey Dell's main concern is with an abortion.

But Dewey Dell is also a comic figure. Her actions and her thoughts are constantly compared to the slow deliberate movement of a cow. She approaches life with the quietness and peacefulness of an animal. Her willingness to go to the cellar with the druggist in Jefferson shows her naive yet knowing qualities, as if she knew that it wouldn't help with the abortion, but thought that it was an experience anyway. The only time that she is moved to action is when she attacks Darl at the grave, and this attack is prompted by her fear of him.

VARDAMAN

Vardaman's age is never given in the novel. He is younger than Dewey Dell, who is seventeen. Most readers seem to think of Vardaman as being between twelve and fourteen, but other readers choose to view him as a much younger boy of six or seven. There is evidence to support both views.

In Addie's statement that she "gave Anse Dewey Dell to negative Jewel. Then I gave him Vardaman to replace the child I robbed him of," the implication is that Vardaman's birth followed soon after Dewey Dell's. Thus if Dewey Dell is seventeen, Vardaman would be only a couple of years younger. Furthermore when someone is needed to go after Dr. Peabody's runaway team, it seems more logical for them to send a fourteen-year-old than it would be to send a seven-year-old. Finally, there are suggestions that Addie is about fifty-three at her death. If Vardaman is only seven, that would mean she gave birth at age forty-six or forty-seven, which, technically speaking, is not impossible but is highly improbable.

In support of Vardaman's being younger, Faulkner himself in *Faulkner at the University* refers to Vardaman as a "child." Several images suggest that he is a very young person. For example, the fish he caught is almost as big as he is and there are few fish in Mississippi ponds almost as large as a fourteen-year-old boy. Furthermore, when he is standing at Tull's door, he cannot be seen by the adult man, suggesting that he is rather small.

In general, Vardaman's actions, such as boring a hole in his mother's coffin, suggest that he is either a young boy incapable of understanding death or that he is a retarded fourteen-year-old.

FAULKNER'S STYLE AND IMAGERY

Faulkner's style in this novel varies according to the character who is narrating the section. The subtle variations in the style are one of the notable achievements of this novel. There is not a glaring and abrupt change from section to section; there is still the continuity of the same author behind each section, but there is enough variation to make each narrator distinctly different.

The technique that Faulkner uses in many of the sections is called the "stream-of-consciousness" technique. Prior to the twentieth century, an author would simply tell the reader what one of the characters was thinking. Stream-of-consciousness is a technique whereby the author writes as though he is inside the mind of the characters. Since the ordinary person's mind jumps from one event to another, stream-of-consciousness tries to capture this phenomenon. Thus in many sections, notably in the Vardaman and Darl sections, everything is presented through an apparently unorganized succession of images.

Each of the fifty-nine sections in this novel, therefore, represents the inner thought of the character who is narrating the section. This technique reflects the twentieth-century development, research, and interest in the psychology of "free association" and the inner thoughts of man. As a technique, stream-of-consciousness was popularized by James Joyce and Virginia Woolf. But Faulkner's use of this technique is probably the most successful and outstanding use that we have yet had. Even while using this technique, Faulkner varies it enough so as to capture the essence of each character.

Darl is the most complicated character in the novel. And so his sections reflect a mind that is contemplating the intricacies of life. The style is more complicated and the presentation is essentially through poetic imagery. From Darl we receive views of the other characters that penetrate into the very heart of that character. And these views are often expressed with an acute eye for detail. Thus Darl's sections are complicated and the most difficult to penetrate because Darl is the most complex character and his thought process is the most involved.

But Cash's sections are quite different. Cash can think of only one thing at a time. While he is building the coffin, he can realize no other concept. Therefore, his narration is exceptionally simple and is captured in the section where he lists in thirteen steps exactly how he is building the coffin. Thus, whereas Darl was a complicated character and his resulting narration was complicated, Cash's narration is extremely simplified because Cash can handle only one thought at one time.

Dewey Dell's narration is again quite different. She says that she wishes she could worry but she also confesses that she can't think about anything long enough to worry about it. Since she is so basic, so earthy, and so elemental that she can't think about one thing very long, her sections seem to jump from one thought to another. The closest that she comes to logical thought is when she tries to reason about her own seduction. Therefore Faulkner adapts his style to presenting a careless, elementary woman who functions only on a physical level.

With Vardaman, we have another type of difficulty. Faulkner wanted to show us the confused mind of a retarded youth. In order to convince the reader that Vardaman was able to confuse his mother with a fish, Faulkner had to show a mind that jumped from one thought to another. He tried to show how one association led to another rather similar association. There are no difficult words because the mind of a retarded boy would naturally be simple. But the sections are not simple. Since this mind does not function logically, Faulkner records the mind's thinking in terms of basic images. For the most part, these images involve the death of the fish, the death of his mother, being caught in a barn and being unable to breathe. Gradually these associations are made into one image with the resultant statement by Vardaman: "My mother is a fish." Thus Faulkner has achieved a stylistic success by suggesting the functioning within the mind of a retarded person, but has still brought enough order to that mind so that the reader can follow his thoughts.

In Jewel's one section, Faulkner has Jewel contemplating mute acts of violence. This is a mind that can express itself only through acts of violence and thus Jewel narrates only one section.

Addie's section is narrated in terse, cryptic, and expository prose because Addie is a person who has tried to solve some of the basic problems of life and has failed. Therefore, she tends only to state her views in rather direct terms, especially since she maintains that words are useless.

Anse's sections reveal the hypocrisy of the man and furthermore comically reveal how he has deluded himself into thinking himself sincere. He narrates his sections rather simply and in a chronological order because he is not concerned with anything except that which affects his own person.

The outside narrators all function to enlighten some aspect of the Bundren world or to fill in with some factual material. Thus the outside narrators all present their sections without any degree of complication. Each varies according to the personality of the narrator. For example, Cora Tull expresses herself in terms of superficial religious imagery, and Dr. Peabody expresses himself in terms of blunt, sarcastic accusations.

So Faulkner's virtuosity is seen by the way he adjusts his style to fit the mind of each individual narrator. From Darl's poetic observation to Vardaman's confused associations to Cash's literal-mindedness, Faulkner's style shifts in order to lend additional support to his subject matter.

REVIEW QUESTIONS

1. Why does Faulkner use so many individual narrators?

2. What is gained by using so many separate narrators?

3. Why are many scenes narrated by people outside the Bundren Family?

4. Why does Jewel narrate only one short section?

5. Why does Vardaman confuse his mother with a fish?

6. How is this pathetic confusion made comic later on?

7. Why does Addie's section come in the middle of the journey after she has been dead for several days?

8. Addie maintains that words are useless. How is this concept supported by Anse and the preacher Whitfield?

66

9. Other than the fact that Cash is a good carpenter, why is he chosen to build the coffin?

10. Why is Darl used to narrate most of the sections, particularly the ones where some important event is occurring?

11. Why does Dewey Dell hate Darl so intensely?

12. What is the meaning of Darl's taunt "Jewel's mother is a horse"?

THEME TOPICS

1. Write an essay proving that Darl is sane.

2. Give as much support as possible to the proposition that seen against the Bundren world, Darl is insane.

3. Write a theme defining Addie's relationship to her children.

4. Write a theme discussing how the comic aspects of the novel help modify the grotesque or horrible aspects of the journey.

5. Using this novel as your basis, distinguish between scenes which are comic and pathetic, or between the tragic and the grotesque. Cite as many specific examples as possible.

6. Explain the purpose of the outside narrator. Does this purpose remain the same throughout the novel?

7. Develop Darl's relationship to Addie, to Anse, and to the other members of the family.

8. Write an essay showing Darl as the defeated idealist.

SELECTED BIBLIOGRAPHY

BACKMAN, MELVIN. *Faulkner: The Major Years: A Critical Study.* Bloomington: Indiana University Press, 1966. The chief value of this study is that it gives many of the prominent critical theories about the major novels.

BROOKS, CLEANTH. *William Faulkner: The Yoknapatawpha Novels.* Yale, 1963. One of the outstanding studies on Faulkner, it has a section at the back filled with many individual insights into individual problems.

CAMPBELL, HARRY M., and RUEL E. FOSTER. *William Faulkner.* Norman: University of Oklahoma Press, 1953. One of the earlier studies, it is useful as a basic guide from which other critics evolved their theories.

CULLEN, JOHN B., and FLOYD C. WATKINS. *Old Times in the Faulkner Country.* Chapel Hill: The University of North Carolina Press, 1961.

FAULKNER, WILLIAM. *Faulkner in the University,* ed. FREDERICK L. GWYNN, and JOSEPH L. BLOTNER. Charlottesville: University of Virginia, 1959. A series of taped questions put to Faulkner by students at the University of Virginia along with Faulkner's answers.

HOFFMAN, FREDERICK, and OLGA VICKERY (eds.). *William Faulkner: Three Decades of Criticism.* East Lansing: Michigan State University Press, 1960. A collection of some of the best essays written on Faulkner. A very valuable reference book.

HOFFMAN, FREDERICK. *William Faulkner.* New York: Twayne Publishers, 1961. A basic introduction to Faulkner as a writer.

HOWE, IRVING. *William Faulkner: A Critical Study.* New York: Random House, 1952. A general interpretation that gives a broad view of Faulkner even though there is a deficiency of "in depth" criticism.

HUNT, JOHN W[ESLEY]. *William Faulkner: Art in Theological Tension.* Syracuse, N.Y.: Syracuse University Press, 1965.

LONGLEY, JOHN LEWIS, JR. *The Tragic Mask: A Study of Faulkner's Heroes.* Chapel Hill: University of North Carolina Press, 1963.

MALIN, IRVING. *William Faulkner, an Interpretation.* Stanford: Stanford University Press, 1957.

MILLGATE, MICHAEL. *William Faulkner.* New York: Grove Press, 1961. A useful introduction, particularly for the beginning student of Faulkner.

MINER, WARD L. *The World of William Faulkner.* New York: Grove Press, 1959. A brief account of Faulkner's family and the Mississippi environment.

O'CONNOR, WILLIAM VAN. *The Tangled Fire of William Faulkner.* Minneapolis: University of Minnesota Press, 1960. Contains many excellent chapters even though some chapters on some novels deal with a rather specific aspect of the novel.

RUNYAN, HARRY A. *A Faulkner Glossary.* New York: Citadel Press, 1964.

SLATOFF, WALTER J. *Quest for Failure: A Study of William Faulkner.* Ithaca, N.Y.: Cornell University Press, 1960.

SWIGGART, PETER. *The Art of Faulkner's Novels.* Austin: University of Texas Press, 1962. One of the best studies of Faulkner's major novels, it discusses the greatness of Faulkner's art.

THOMPSON, LAWRENCE. *William Faulkner: An Introduction and Interpretation.* New York: Barnes and Noble, 1963. Perhaps the best short study yet to appear on Faulkner, this volume brings together many of the obvious critical views about Faulkner.

VICKERY, OLGA W. *The Novels of William Faulkner.* Baton Rouge: Louisiana Press, 1959. Perhaps the finest book yet to appear on Faulkner. Mrs. Vickery handles most of Faulkner's fiction in depth.

WAGGONER, HYATT H. *William Faulkner: From Jefferson to the World.* Lexington: University of Kentucky Press, 1959.

WARREN, ROBERT PENN (ed.). *Faulkner: A Collection of Critical Essays.* Englewood Cliffs, N.J.: Prentice Hall, 1966.

WAGGONER, HYATT H. *William Faulkner: From Jefferson to the World.* Lexington: University of Kentucky Press, 1959.

NOTES

Your Guides to Successful Test Preparation.

Cliffs Test Preparation Guides

Efficient preparation means better test scores. Go with the experts and use **Cliffs Test Preparation Guides.** They'll help you reach your goals because they're: Complete • Concise • Functional • In-depth. They are focused on helping you know what to expect from each test. The test-taking techniques have been proven in classroom programs nationwide.

Recommended for individual use or as a part of formal test preparation programs.

TITLES	QTY.
2068-8 **ENHANCED ACT ($5.95)**	
2030-0 **CBEST ($7.95)**	
2040-8 **CLAST ($8.95)**	
1471-8 **ESSAY EXAM ($4.95)**	
2031-9 **ELM Review ($6.95)**	
2060-2 **GMAT ($7.95)**	
2008-4 **GRE ($6.95)**	
2065-3 **LSAT ($7.95)**	
2033-5 **MATH Review for Standardized Tests ($8.95)**	
2017-3 **NTE Core Battery ($14.95)**	
2020-3 **Memory Power for Exams ($4.95)**	
2044-0 **Police Sergeant Examination Preparation Guide ($9.95)**	
2032-7 **PPST ($7.95)**	
2002-5 **PSAT/NMSQT ($4.50)**	
2000-9 **SAT ($5.95)**	
2042-4 **TASP ($7.95)**	
2018-1 **TOEFL w/cassette ($14.95)**	
2034-3 **VERBAL Review for Standardized Tests ($7.95)**	
2041-6 **You Can Pass the GED ($9.95)**	

Prices subject to change without notice.
Available at your local bookseller or order by sending
the coupon with your check. **Cliffs Notes, Inc.,**
P.O. Box 80728, Lincoln, NE 68501.

Name _____
Address _____
City _____
State _____ **Zip** _____

P.O. Box 80728, Lincoln, NE 68501